Afloat with a Musical Goat

And Other Silly Limericks for Kids

By
Julie Miller

Harmonic
PRESS
Ormond Beach, Florida

Published by Harmonic Press
An imprint of Miller Math, Inc.
Ormond Beach, FL

ISBN: 978-0-9978707-4-9
Library of Congress Control Number: 2017900782

First Harmonic Press printing: January 2017

Afloat with a Musical Goat

I once knew a musical goat,

Who traveled afloat in a boat.

As she floated along,

She'd sing all day long

Until she sustained a sore throat.

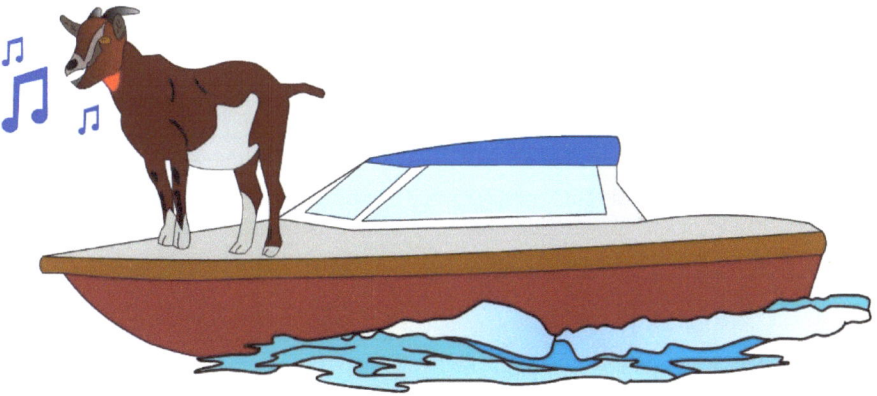

The Smell of Old Socks

I once knew a T-Rex named Ox.

His breath smelled as bad as a croc's.

His arms wouldn't reach

To brush his big teeth,

So his breath had the smell of old socks.

Whom Do We See in the Tree?

A girl of age three, up in a tree

Was hanging by arm and by knee.

A bit of a clown,

She hung upside

down,

Like a monkey or

small chimpanzee.

Down the Right Path

A girl once had trouble with math.

She grumbled with venomous wrath.

But she opened
her book,
And took a
quick look,

And her logic
went down
the right path.

Too Cool for School

A girl was too cool and hated her school.

A bit of a fool, she broke every rule.

She paid
  no attention,

And went
  to detention,

Then stayed after school...how un-cool.

Healthy Louise

I once knew a girl

    named Louise,

Who ate nothing but

    pizza with cheese.

But for reasons of health,

She said to herself,

"I need to eat spinach and peas."

A Tiger Who Sings

There once was a tiger named Stripes,

Who sang with a great set of pipes.

And loudly he sang,

An ear-splitting twang,

Yee Haw
You'all

Leaving all who could

   hear him

   with gripes.

Rain Comes with Rainbows

There are flowers and rainbows in May,

And Frank wants to go out and play.

But take an umbrella,

Or be a wet fella,

'Cause rain comes with rainbows in May.

No Fun Being Sick

I once spent a week being sick,

As though I'd been hit by a brick.

I sneezed from my nose,

To the tips of my toes.

I need some more tissue real quick.

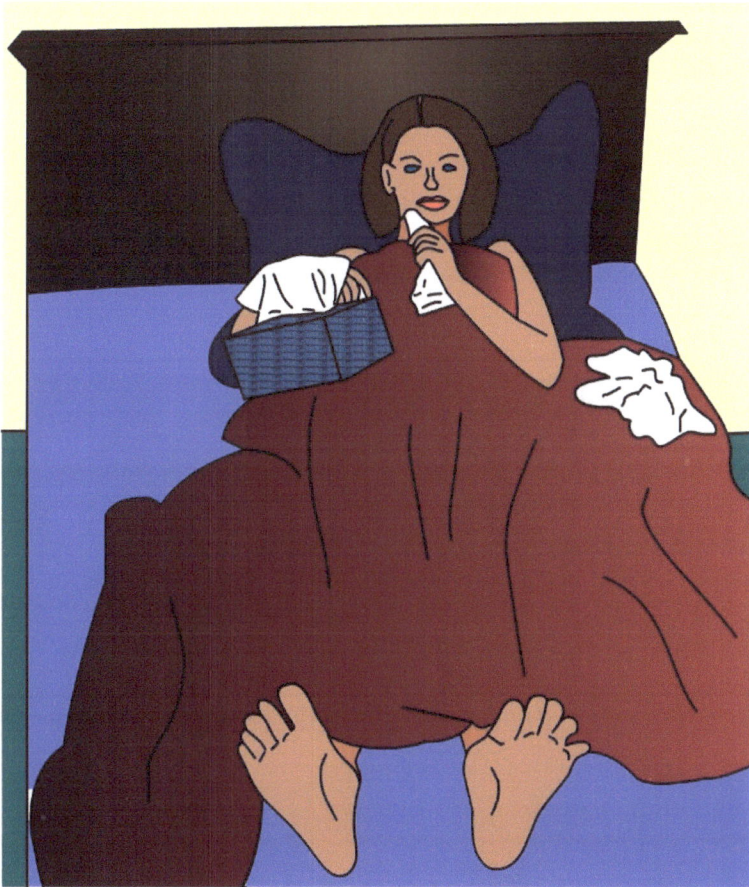

Frightening Thunder and Lightning

The sky became dark like a bruise,

With winds and big clouds of chartreuse.

The thunder and lightning

Were terribly frightening,

And the rain made us bring out canoes.

A Nerd, A Cow, and a Bird

There once was a farmer named Nerd,

Whose eyes saw a thing quite absurd.

A cow came along,

Singing a song,

While toting a tropical bird.

The Pet Squirrel of Earl

There once was a student named Earl,
Who lived with a bushy pet squirrel.
Its curly brown tail,
Was as big as a whale,
And looked like a tight spiral curl.

Who Chases Whom?

A cat chased a bird with great glee.

The bird then flew up in a tree.

A dog chased the cat.

The cat promptly scat,

And ran up the

tree like a flea.

A Bad Lad Who's Sad

There once was
a very bad lad.
He stole from his
very own dad.

And sometimes
he swore,
And stole from
the poor,

Then lived in a jail
and felt sad.

Sundaes with Spinach Soufflé

It's Sunday and sunny today,

A great day to go out and play,

To run in the sun,

Then eat something fun,

Like sundaes and spinach soufflé.

Tigers with Visors

Two tigers escaped from the zoo.

The grown-ups said, "What should we do?

What if the tigers

Put on some visors

And go to the beach to eat you?"

Poor Nell Can't Spell

We once had a teacher named Nell,

Who didn't quite know how to spell.

She couldn't spell "snakes,"

We called her "Miss Steaks,"

Then we taught her to spell, which was swell.

A Cat, and a Rat in a Hat

Patty the cat found a big rat
And chased it right into a hat.

The hat was put on,
Surprised poor old John,

Who fainted right
   there where he sat.

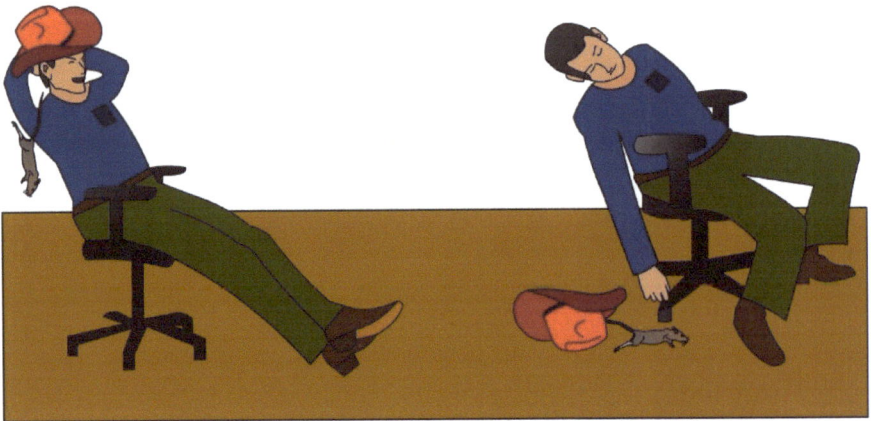

Stand Up Against Mac

There once was a
  bully named Mac,
Who shoved a young
  kid on his back.

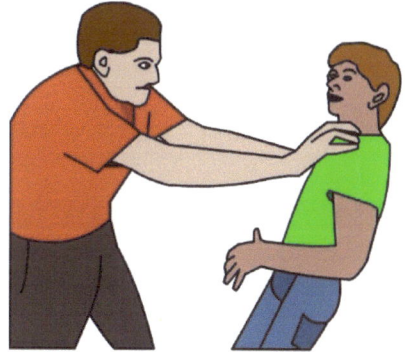

So others around,
All stood their ground,
To save the young kid from attack.

A Kite Taking Flight

A kid at the beach, flying a kite,

The kite was a sight, taking its flight.

The wind came on hard,

The boy was on guard,

As he pulled back with all of his might.

Tim at the Gym

There once was an athlete named Tim,

Who liked to work out at the gym.

But pull-ups and sit-ups
Brought on the hiccups

That left him to shake
from each limb.

No Leaves on the Trees

There once was a
   farmer named Jeeves,
Who lived off the
   coast of Belize.

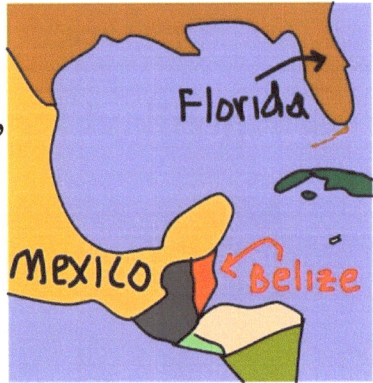

While raking some leaves,

He let out a sneeze,

And blew all the leaves from the trees.

Running too Young

There once was a
   boy of age one,
Who wanted to
   learn how to run.

He tilted and tipped,
And finally he slipped,

For he was a bit still too young.

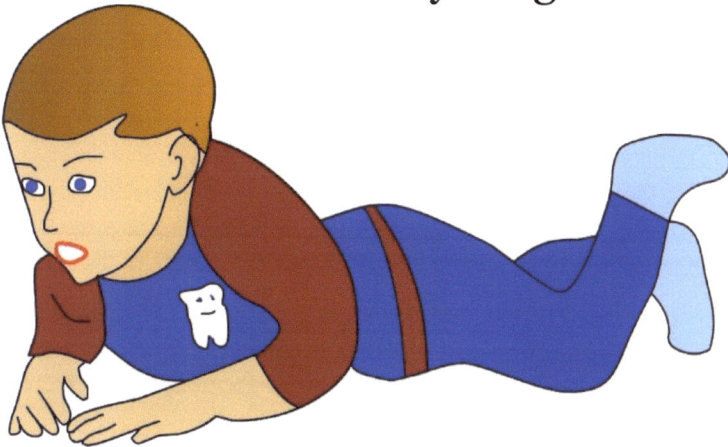

Swim Like a Goose, Smell Like a Spruce

"To bathe, you see, what is the use?

Instead I shall swim like a goose.

If I do not bathe,

More water we'll save,

And I'll be as fresh as a spruce."

About Limericks

A **limerick** is a short, 5-line poem with the following rhyming pattern.

- The first, second, and fifth lines rhyme.
- The third and fourth lines rhyme.

A limerick typically has 34 syllables and tells a surprising, humorous story using a musical beat. The **meter** (or rhythm) of a limerick has the following structure.

The syllable "Da" (with a capital "D") represents a strong stress, and "da" (with lower case "d") represents a weak stress.

1. da Da da da Da da da DA
2. da DA da da Da da da DA
3. da DA da da DA
4. da Da da da DA
5. da Da da da Da da da DA

Make Your Own Limerick

Try making your own limerick. In the practice examples below, the first line is already given. For Example 1, think of words that rhyme with "Fred" (such as "red," "bed," "bread," "said," "instead," and so on). This will help you form the second and fifth lines of the limerick.

Practice:

Example 1.   There once was a fellow named Fred.

Example 2.   There once was a girl on the run.

About the Author

Julie Miller is the author of several short works of fiction and non-fiction for young readers and the author of nine textbooks in mathematics. As a former math teacher, Julie values education as part of an interesting and robust life. While she loves mathematics, she recognizes that reading is the foundation of all learning. She hopes that this silly book of limericks will be part of a nightly ritual of bedtime stories for many families. Julie lives in Florida with her fabulous black-and-white cat, Sine.

www.ingramcontent.com/pod-product-compliance
Lightning Source LLC
Chambersburg PA
CBHW041756050426
42443CB00023B/20